In the Year 1992

by

Kerry Butters.

In the Year 1992

Millennium:	2nd millennium
Centuries:	19th century – **20th century** – 21st century
Decades:	1960s 1970s 1980s – **1990s** – 2000s 2010s 2020s
Years:	1989 1990 1991 – **1992** – 1993 1994 1995

1992 (MCMXCII) was a leap year starting on Wednesday (dominical letter ED) of the Gregorian calendar, the 1992nd year of the Common Era (CE) and *Anno Domini* (AD) designations, the 992nd year of the 2nd millennium, the 92nd year of the 20th century, and the 3rd year of the 1990s decade.

1992 designated as:

International Space Year by the United Nations.

Contents

Events

January

- January 1
  - The Atari 2600 is finally discontinued 15 years after its introduction in September 1977.
  - Boutros Boutros-Ghali of Egypt replaces Javier Pérez de Cuéllar of Peru as United Nations Secretary-General.
  - George H. W. Bush becomes the first U.S. President to address the Australian Parliament.
- January 2 – President of Russia Boris Yeltsin ends price controls, resulting in prices of some goods and services becoming 3 to 5 times more expensive. This in effect ends the command economy in Russia.
- January 6 – The Nagorno-Karabakh Republic is proclaimed by the Armenians of Nagorno-Karabakh.
- January 7 – The Yugoslav Air Force downs a helicopter, killing 5 military observers from the European Community.
- January 8 – George H. W. Bush is televised falling violently ill at a state dinner in Japan, vomiting into the lap of Prime Minister Kiichi Miyazawa and fainting.
- January 9 – Bosnian Serbs declare their own republic within Bosnia and Herzegovina, in protest of the decision by Bosniaks and Bosnian Croats to seek EC recognition.
- January 11
  - Singer Paul Simon is the first major artist to tour South Africa after the end of the cultural boycott.

- o Shanda Sharer is tortured and burned to death in Madison, Indiana by 4 teenage girls.
- January 12 – The second round of Algeria's general elections is cancelled when the first round is favorable to the Islamic Salvation Front.
- January 13 – Japan apologizes for forcing Korean women into sexual slavery during World War II.
- January 15 – The Socialist Federal Republic of Yugoslavia begins to break up. Slovenia and Croatia gain independence and international recognition in some Western countries.
- January 16 – El Salvador officials and rebel leaders sign the Chapultepec Peace Accords in Mexico City ending the 12-year Salvadoran Civil War that claimed at least 75,000 lives.
- January 18 – In Nairobi, Kenya, more than 100,000 attend protests demanding an end to one-party rule by the Kenya African National Union.
- January 19
  - o The Bulgarian presidential election is won by Zhelyu Zhelev, leader of the Union of Democratic Forces.
  - o Paramount Leader of China Deng Xiaoping speaks in Shenzhen during his southern tour, a move that would return China on its right-wing march towards free market economics.
- January 20 – Cuba executes Eduardo Diaz Betancourt, who was found guilty of sabotage and terrorism.
- January 21 – Faced with decreased military spending, United Technologies Corporation announces it will eliminate 13,900 jobs by 1993.
- January 22
  - o Rebel forces occupy Zaire's national radio station in Kinshasa and broadcast a demand for the government's resignation.
  - o *STS-42*: Dr. Roberta Bondar becomes the first Canadian woman in space, aboard Space Shuttle *Discovery*.
- January 24
  - o In El Salvador, an army colonel and a lieutenant of the Atlacatl Battalion are each sentenced to 30 years in prison for the 1989 murder of six Jesuit priests and their housekeepers.

- China and Israel establish diplomatic relations.
- January 26
  - Boris Yeltsin announces that Russia will stop targeting cities of the United States and her allies with nuclear weapons. In return George H. W. Bush announces that the United States and her allies will stop targeting Russia and the remaining communist states with nuclear weapons.
  - In Mauritania, security forces open fire on opponents of President of Mauritania Maaouya Ould Sid'Ahmed Taya, killing at least 5 people.
- January 27
  - Macy's files for bankruptcy.
  - Nagorno-Karabakh War: in the disputed territory of Nagorno-Karabakh, fighting between Armenians and Azeris leaves at least 60 people dead.
- January 30 – North Korea signs an accord with the International Atomic Energy Agency allowing for international inspections of North Korea's nuclear power plants.
- January 31 – The heads of state of the 5 permanent members of the United Nations Security Council, and of most of the temporary members, meet in New York City to discuss the new world order in the post-Cold War world.

February

- February 1
  - President of the United States George H. W. Bush meets with President of Russia Boris Yeltsin at Camp David, where they formally declare that the Cold War is over.
  - The United States Coast Guard begins deporting the first of some 14,000 refugees from Haiti.
- February 4 – In Venezuela, Hugo Chávez leads an unsuccessful coup attempt against President of Venezuela Carlos Andrés Pérez.
- February 6 – The United States Senate approves a measure calling for the faster phase-out of chlorofluorocarbons under the revised Montreal Protocol; the phase-out is later completed in 2000.

- February 7 – The Maastricht Treaty is signed, founding the European Union.
- February 8 – The opening ceremony for the 1992 Winter Olympics is held in Albertville, France.
- February 9 – Algerian Civil War: The government of Algeria declares a state of emergency and begins a crackdown on the Islamic Salvation Front.
- February 10 – Boxer Mike Tyson, the former undisputed heavyweight champion of the world, is found guilty of raping 18-year-old Desiree Washington, Miss Black Rhode Island, by a jury in Indianapolis. On March 26, he is sentenced to 6 years in prison.
- February 11 – An F-16 jet crashes into a residential district of Hengelo, the Netherlands; no casualties are reported.
- February 14 – Ukraine and 4 other nations in the Commonwealth of Independent States reject Russia's proposal to maintain unified armed forces. Ukraine, Moldova, and Azerbaijan announce they will go ahead with plans to create their own armed forces.
- February 16 – In Lebanon, Israeli helicopter gunships assassinate Abbas al-Musawi, the leader of Hezbollah, and his son, in retaliation for a February 14 raid that killed 3 Israeli soldiers.
- February 17 – A court in Milwaukee, Wisconsin sentences serial killer Jeffrey Dahmer to life in prison.
- February 18
  - Iraq disarmament crisis: The Executive Chairman of UNSCOM details Iraq's refusal to abide by UN Security Council disarmament resolutions.
  - The New Hampshire primary is won by Paul Tsongas on the Democratic side; for the Republicans, Pat Buchanan has a surprisingly strong showing (37%) against incumbent president George H. W. Bush.
- February 21 – The United Nations Security Council approves Resolution 743 to send a UNPROFOR peacekeeping force to Yugoslavia.
- February 23 – The closing ceremony of the 1992 Winter Olympics is held in Albertville.
- February 25 – February 26 – 613 Azerbaijani civilians are massacred in Khojaly.

- February 26 – The Supreme Court of Ireland rules that a 14-year-old rape victim may travel to England to have an abortion.
- February 27 – In Albuquerque, New Mexico, 79-year-old Stella Liebeck is burned by a cup of coffee at a McDonald's located near the city.

March

- Douglas Adams completes Mostly Harmless, the last book in the Hitchhiker's Guide to the Galaxy series.
- March 1 – The first victims of the Bosnian War are a Serb groom's father and an Orthodox priest in a Sarajevo shooting. The Bosnian independence referendum was held from February 29–March 1, in which the majority of the Bosniak and Bosnian Croat communities, boycotted by the Bosnian Serbs, voted for the Yugoslav republic's independence.
- March 3 – Turkey's worst coal mine disaster leaves 263 dead near Zonguldak.
- March 4 – The Supreme Court of Algeria bans the Islamic Salvation Front, which is poised to win control of the Parliament of Algeria in runoff elections.
- March 9 – The People's Republic of China ratifies the Nuclear Non-Proliferation Treaty.
- March 10 – Following Super Tuesday voting, Bill Clinton is declared the likely winner of the Democratic Party presidential primaries.
- March 11 – Manuel de Dios Unanue, former editor of *El Diario La Prensa*, is slain in a restaurant in Queens, New York after having received death threats from the Colombian drug cartels.
- March 12 – Mauritius becomes a republic while remaining a member of the Commonwealth of Nations.
- March 13 – The 6.7 Mw Erzincan earthquake affects eastern Turkey with a maximum Mercalli intensity of VIII (*Severe*), killing 498–652, and injuring around 2,000.
- March 16 – President Boris Yeltsin announces the creation of a separate Russian army, leading to questions about the viability of the Commonwealth of Independent States.

- March 18 – White South Africans vote in favour of political reforms which will end the apartheid regime and create a power-sharing multi-racial government.
- March 19
  - Paul Tsongas withdraws from the Democratic Party presidential primaries, virtually assuring a victory for Bill Clinton.
  - Dow Corning announces that it will stop manufacturing silicone breast implants.
- March 22
  - In French regional elections, the conservative Rally for the Republic and the centre-right Union for French Democracy win in a landslide, capturing 20 of 22 metropolitan regional presidencies.
  - STS-45: Space Shuttle *Atlantis* takes off from Cape Canaveral carrying instruments designed to study global warming.
- March 24 – The Open Skies Treaty is signed in Helsinki, Finland to establish a program of unarmed survelliance flights over the 34 member states. It went into effect on January 1, 2002.
- March 25
  - The International Atomic Energy Agency orders Iraq to destroy an industrial complex at Al Atheer that is being used to manufacture nuclear weapons.
  - Pakistan beats England to win the Cricket World Cup for the very first time.
- March 29 – In France, police arrest 3 men believed to be planning a Basque separatist terrorist attack at the 1992 Summer Olympics.
- March 31 – The Maintenance of Religious Harmony Act of Singapore comes into force.

April

- April 5
  - The Assembly of Bosnia and Herzegovina (without the presence of Serb political delegates) proclaims independence from the Socialist Federal Republic of Yugoslavia.

- Bosnian War: Serb troops, following a mass rebellion of Serbs in Bosnia and Herzegovina against the Bosnian declaration of independence from Yugoslavia, besiege the city of Sarajevo.
  - Approximately 500,000 people march on Washington, D. C. in support of abortion rights in advance of oral arguments in the case of *Planned Parenthood v. Casey*.
  - President of Peru Alberto Fujimori issues Decree Law 25418, dissolving the Congress of the Republic of Peru, imposing censorship and having opposition politicians arrested, setting off the 1992 Peruvian constitutional crisis.
- April 6
  - *Barney & Friends* makes its debut on PBS.
  - Microsoft releases Windows 3.1.
- April 7 – The United States recognizes the independence of Croatia, Bosnia and Herzegovina, and Slovenia. The European Community also recognizes Bosnia and Herzegovina.
- April 9
  - A Miami jury convicts former Panamanian ruler Manuel Noriega of assisting Colombia's cocaine cartel.
  - The United Kingdom general election is narrowly won by the Conservative Party led by Prime Minister of the United Kingdom John Major.
- April 10 – A Provisional Irish Republican Army bomb explodes in the Baltic Exchange in the City of London; 3 are killed, 91 injured.
- April 12 – The *Euro Disney Resort* officially opens with its theme park *Euro Disneyland*. The resort and its park's name are later changed to Disneyland Paris.
- April 13 – The 5.3 Mw Roermond earthquake affects Netherlands, Germany, and Belgium with a maximum Mercalli intensity of VII (*Very strong*).
- April 15 – The National Assembly of Vietnam adopts the 1992 Constitution of the Socialist Republic of Vietnam.
- April 16 – President of Afghanistan Mohammad Najibullah is ousted and detained by Muslim rebels moving towards Kabul, setting the stage for the civil war in Afghanistan (1992–96).
-

- April 20
  - Seville, Spain's 6-month Universal Exhibition, called Seville Expo '92, opens.
  - The Freddie Mercury Tribute Concert, held at Wembley Stadium, is televised live to over 1 billion people and raises millions of dollars for AIDS research.
- April 21 – The death of Grand Duke Vladimir Kirillovich of Russia results in a succession dispute between Nicholas Romanov, Prince of Russia and Vladimir's daughter Maria for the leadership of the Imperial Family of Russia.
- April 22 – Fuel that leaked into a sewer explodes in Guadalajara, Mexico; 215 are killed, 1,500 injured.
- April 27 – Betty Boothroyd becomes the first woman elected Speaker of the British House of Commons.
- April 28 – The two remaining constituent republics of the former Socialist Federal Republic of Yugoslavia – Serbia and Montenegro – form a new state, named the Federal Republic of Yugoslavia (after 2003, Serbia and Montenegro), bringing to an end the official union of Serbs, Croats, Slovenes, Montenegrins, Bosnian Muslims and Macedonians that existed from 1918 (with the exception of the period during World War II).
- April 29 – Los Angeles riots: The acquittal of 4 police officers in the Rodney King beating criminal trial triggers massive rioting in Los Angeles. The riots will last for 6 days resulting in 53 deaths and over a $1 billion in damages before order is restored.

May

- May 5 – Russian leaders in Crimea declare their separation from Ukraine as a new republic. They withdraw the secession on May 10.
- May 7
  - STS-49: Space Shuttle *Endeavour* makes its maiden flight, as a replacement for Space Shuttle *Challenger*.
  - The Michigan Legislature approves the Twenty-seventh Amendment to the United States Constitution. With that

approval, the amendment had been adopted by 38 states and is thereby approved.

- o The Sydney River McDonald's murders in Nova Scotia, Canada got international attention as three employees where killed and a fourth was left permanently disabled during a botched robbery. It was the first fast food restaurant murders in Canada.
- May 9 – The United Nations Framework Convention on Climate Change is adopted in New York.
- May 10 – Sweden wins the Ice Hockey World Championships in Czechoslovakia defeating Finland, 5-2, in the final game in Prague.
- May 12 – The United States recalls United States Ambassador to Yugoslavia Warren Zimmermann, to protest military aggression against Bosnia and Hercegovina.
- May 13 – Falun Gong is introduced by Li Hongzhi in China.
- May 14 – Australia's longest running travel TV show *Getaway* airs on Nine Network.
- May 15
    - o The Commonwealth of Independent States Collective Security Treaty (CST) is signed (effective 20 April 1994).
    - o The Genoa Expo '92 World's Fair opens in Genoa, Italy.
- May 16 – *STS-49*: Space Shuttle *Endeavour* lands safely after a successful maiden voyage.
- May 16–17 – Bosnian War: U.N. peacekeepers withdraw from Sarajevo.
- May 17 – Protests begin in Bangkok, Thailand, against the government of General Suchinda Kraprayoon, sparking a bloody crackdown.
- May 18 – The Twenty-seventh Amendment to the United States Constitution is enacted.
- May 22 – The Tonight Show Starring Johnny Carson airs its final show on NBC.
- May 23 – A Mafia bomb kills Italian anti-Mafia judge Giovanni Falcone.

- May 24
  - In Thailand, Suchinda Kraprayoon agrees to resign.
  - Serbian irregulars kill at least 16 people on a bread line in Sarajevo.
- May 25 – In Australia, Lindy Chamberlain receives compensation for wrongful conviction on murder charges.
- May 26 – Charles Geschke, President of Adobe Systems, is kidnapped from his company parking lot. The kidnappers demand $650,000 ransom; they are later apprehended.
- May 30 – United Nations Security Council Resolution 757 imposes economic sanctions on Yugoslavia in an effort to end its attacks on Bosnia and Hercegovina.
- May 31 – Evan Fong, Canadian YouTube celebrity

June

- June 2 – In a national referendum Denmark rejects the Maastricht Treaty by a narrow margin.
- June 8 – The first World Ocean Day is celebrated, coinciding with the Earth Summit held in Rio de Janeiro, Brazil.
- June 16
  - A 'Joint Understanding' agreement on arms reduction is signed by U.S. President George H. W. Bush and Russian President Boris Yeltsin (this is later codified in START II).
  - A federal grand jury indicts Caspar Weinberger for his role in covering up the Iran–Contra affair.
- June 17 – Two German relief workers held since 1989, Thomas Kemptner and Heinrich Struebig, are released (they are the last Western hostages in Lebanon).
- June 20 – Estonia adopts the kroon and becomes the first former Soviet Republic to replace the Soviet ruble.
- June 21 – Nelson Mandela announces that the African National Congress will halt negotiations with the government of South Africa following the Boipatong massacre of June 17.
- June 22 – Two skeletons excavated in Yekaterinburg are identified as Tsar Nicholas II of Russia and Tsarina Alexandra.
-

- June 23
  - The Israeli legislative election is won by the Israeli Labor Party under the leadership of Yitzhak Rabin, ousting a Likud government.
  - Gambino crime family boss John Gotti is sentenced to life without parole for the murder of Paul Castellano and other crimes.
- June 25 – The Black Sea Economic Cooperation (BSEC) is founded.
- June 26
  - Denmark beats Germany 2–0 to win the 1992 UEFA European Football Championship at Ullevi Stadium in Gothenburg, Sweden.
  - United States Secretary of the Navy Henry L. Garrett III resigns in the wake of the Tailhook scandal.
- June 28
  - Estonia holds a referendum on its constitution, which will come into effect on July 3.
  - Junko Tabei scales Puncak Jaya to become the first woman to complete the Seven Summits.
- June 29
  - A bodyguard assassinates President Mohamed Boudiaf of Algeria.
  - The Supreme Court of the United States upholds the 1973 decision of *Roe v. Wade* in *Planned Parenthood v. Casey*, a 5-4 decision.

July

- July 4 – Steffi Graf wins the 1992 Wimbledon Championships – Women's Singles. On July 5, Andre Agassi wins the 1992 Wimbledon Championships – Men's Singles.
- July 6–8 – The 18th G7 summit is held in Munich.
- July 6–29 – Iraq disarmament crisis: Iraq refuses a U.N. inspection team access to the Iraqi Ministry of Agriculture. UNSCOM claims that it has reliable information that the site contains archives related to illegal weapons activities. U.N. Inspectors stage a 17-day

"sit-in" outside of the building, but leave when their safety is threatened by Iraqi soldiers.

- July 8 – Amoco and Unocal Corporation announce restructuring plans that will eliminate 10,000 jobs in 1992 and 1993.
- July 9 – Bill Clinton announces his selection of Al Gore as his running mate in the 1992 U.S. presidential election.
- July 10
    - In Miami, former Panamanian leader Manuel Noriega is sentenced to 40 years in prison for drug and racketeering violations.
    - The Giotto spacecraft flies past Comet 26P/Grigg–Skjellerup, gathering measurements about the comet.
- July 13 – Yitzhak Rabin becomes prime minister of Israel.
- July 16
    - Ross Perot announces he is ending his presidential campaign.
    - At the 1992 Democratic National Convention, Arkansas Governor Bill Clinton accepts his party's presidential nomination on behalf of the "forgotten middle class".
- July 17 – The Slovak National Council declares Slovakia an independent country, signaling the breakup of Czechoslovakia.
- July 19
    - A car bomb placed by the Mafia (with the collaboration of Italian intelligence) kills judge Paolo Borsellino and 5 members of his escort.
    - The Cabinet of Israel approves a freeze on new settlements in the occupied territories, a move expected to reinvigorate the Middle East Peace Process.
- July 20
    - Václav Havel resigns as president of Czechoslovakia.
    - An airlift of food and medicine to Sarajevo is halted after 23 days due to renewed fighting.
    - A Bell Boeing V-22 Osprey crashes in the Potomac River as it approaches Marine Corps Base Quantico, killing all 7 people on board.
- July 21 – Transnistria War ends with a ceasefire.

- July 22 – Near Medellín, Colombian drug lord Pablo Escobar escapes from his luxury prison, fearing extradition to the United States.
- July 23 – Abkhazia declares independence from Georgia.
- July 25 – August 9 – The 1992 Summer Olympics are held in Barcelona, Catalonia, Spain.
- July 26 – Iraq agrees to allow U.N. weapons inspectors to search the Iraqi Agricultural Ministry building in Baghdad. When inspectors arrive on July 28 and 29, they find nothing and voice suspicions that Iraqi records had been removed.
- July 31
  - The ex-Soviet Republic of Georgia becomes the 179th member of the United Nations.
  - Thai Airways International Flight 311, an Airbus A310-300, crashes into a mountain north of Kathmandu, Nepal killing all 113 people on board.
  - China General Aviation Flight 7552 bound for Xiamen crashes soon after taking off from Nanjing Dajiaochang Airport, killing 108 of the 116 people on board.

August

- August 3–4 – Millions of black South Africans participate in a general strike called by the African National Congress to protest the lack of progress in negotiations with the government of President of South Africa F. W. de Klerk.
- August 6 – President Bush urges the United Nations to approve a military intervention in Bosnia and Hercegovina.
- August 10 – The UK government bans the Ulster Defence Association, a loyalist paramilitary organisation that had been legal for 20 years.
- August 12 – Canada, Mexico, and the United States announce that a deal has been reached on the North American Free Trade Agreement; the deal will be formally signed on December 17, 1992.
- August 17 – The 1992 Republican National Convention convenes in Houston.

- August 18 – Prime Minister of the United Kingdom John Major announces the creation of the Iraqi no-fly zones.
- August 20 – Kristiansund's connection to the mainland of Norway, Krifast, opens.
- August 21–22 – Events at Ruby Ridge, Idaho, are sparked by a Federal Marshal surveillance team, resulting in the death of a Marshal, Sam Weaver and his dog and the next day the wounding of Randy Weaver, the death of his wife Vicki and the wounding of Kevin Harris.
- August 23 – Hurricane Andrew attains Category 5 status on the Saffir–Simpson hurricane scale, and at 2100 UTC hits Eleuthera and the Bahama Banks.
- August 24
  - A special commission in Brazil concludes that there is sufficient evidence to begin impeachment proceedings against President of Brazil Fernando Collor de Mello, finding he had accepted millions of dollars worth of illegal payments from business interests.
  - China and South Korea establish diplomatic relations.
- August 24 – August 28 – Hurricane Andrew hits south Florida and dissipates over the Tennessee valley when it merges with a storm system; 23 are killed.
- August 29 – In Rostock, Germany, tens of thousands rally to protest neo-Nazi attacks on refugees and immigrants begun on August 22.
- August 30 – The 11-day Ruby Ridge standoff ends with Randy Weaver surrendering to federal authorities.

September

- September 1 – In Beijing, police arrest Shen Tong for his role in organizing the Tiananmen Square protests of 1989.
- September 2 – An earthquake in Nicaragua kills at least 116 people.
- September 7
  - In Ciskei, members of the Ciskei Defence Force loyal to dictator Oupa Gqozo open fire into a crowd of anti-Gqozo

protestors organized by the African National Congress, killing at least 28 people and wounding nearly 200.
- ○ President of Tajikistan Rahmon Nabiyev is forced to resign following weeks of clan and religious warfare that left nearly 2,000 people dead.
- September 11 – Hurricane Iniki hits the Hawaiian Islands, Kauai and Oahu.
- September 12
  - ○ *STS-47*: Dr. Mae Jemison becomes the first African-American woman to travel into space, aboard the Space Shuttle *Endeavour*.
  - ○ In Peru, police arrest Abimael Guzmán, the leader of the Shining Path guerilla movement, who had evaded capture for 12 years.
- September 16 – Black Wednesday: The pound sterling and the Italian lira are forced out of the European Exchange Rate Mechanism.
- September 17 – Two Kurdish opposition leaders are assassinated by the Iranian Kazem Darabi and the Lebanese Abbas Rhayel.
- September 20 – French voters narrowly approve the Maastricht Treaty in the French Maastricht Treaty referendum.
- September 21 – Mexico establishes diplomatic relations with Vatican City, ending a break that lasted over 130 years.
- September 23
  - ○ A large Provisional Irish Republican Army bomb destroys the forensic laboratories in Belfast.
  - ○ Operation Julin is the last nuclear test conducted by the United States at the Nevada Test Site.
- September 28 – Law enforcement officials in the United States, Colombia, and Italy announce that they have arrested more than 165 people on money laundering charges related to cocaine trafficking.
- September 29 – The Chamber of Deputies of Brazil votes to impeach President of Brazil Fernando Collor de Mello, the country's first democratically elected leader in 29 years. Vice President Itamar Franco becomes acting president.

October

- October 1
  - The Cartoon Network is first broadcast on television.
  - Ross Perot reenters the U.S. presidential election.
- October 2 – A riot breaks out in the Carandiru Penitentiary in São Paulo, Brazil, resulting in the Carandiru massacre.
- October 3 – After performing a song protesting alleged child abuse by the Catholic Church, Sinéad O'Connor rips up a photo of Pope John Paul II on *Saturday Night Live*, causing huge controversy, leading the switchboards at NBC to ring off the hook.
- October 4
  - El Al Flight 1862 crashes in Amsterdam, Netherlands; 43 are killed, many more injured.
  - The government of Mozambique signs a truce with leaders of RENAMO, ending the 16-year-old Mozambican Civil War.
- October 6 – Lennart Meri becomes the first President of Estonia after regaining independence. The Estonian Government in Exile resigns on the next day.
- October 7 – In Peru, Shining Path leader Abimael Guzmán is convicted of treason and sentenced to life in prison.
- October 9 – The Chief of Naval Operations adopts the US Navy's core values: Honor, Courage and Commitment.
- October 10 – Tens of thousands rally in Washington, D.C., calling on the government to dedicate more funding to combating HIV/AIDS and unveiling the NAMES Project AIDS Memorial Quilt.
- October 11
  - The *Catechism of the Catholic Church* is promulgated by Pope John Paul II with his apostolic constitution, *Fidei depositum*.
  - President George H. W. Bush, Arkansas Governor Bill Clinton, and Ross Perot participate in the first of 3 televised debates.
- October 12
  - In the Dominican Republic, Pope John Paul II celebrates the 500th anniversary of the meeting of 2 cultures.

- The 1992 Cairo earthquake kills 543 people and injures more than 6,500.
- October 14 – In Japan, Shin Kanemaru of the ruling Liberal Democratic Party resigns over receiving illegal payments from Sagawa Express.
- October 17 – Yoshihiro Hattori, a 16-year-old Japanese exchange student, mistakes the address of a party and is shot dead after knocking on the wrong door in Baton Rouge, Louisiana. The shooter, Rodney Peairs, is later acquitted, sparking outrage in Japan.
- October 19 – The Communist Party of China promotes several market-oriented reformers to the Politburo Standing Committee of the Communist Party of China, signaling a defeat for hard-line ideologues.
- October 21 – Tens of thousands of coal miners march in London to protest government plans to close coal mines and reduce the number of coal miners.
- October 23 – Emperor of Japan Akihito begins the first imperial visit of China, telling a Beijing audience he felt deep sorrow for the suffering of the Chinese people during World War II.
- October 25 – Lithuania holds a referendum on its first constitution after declaring independence from the Soviet Union in 1991.
- October 26 – In a national referendum, voters in Canada reject the Charlottetown Accord.
- October 28 – The end of the world, predicted by the Dami Mission in South Korea, does not occur.
- October 31 – Pope John Paul II issues an apology, and lifts the edict of the Inquisition against Galileo Galilei.

November

- November 3 – United States presidential election, 1992: Arkansas Governor Bill Clinton is elected the 42nd President of the United States.
- November 8 – More than 350,000 people rally in Berlin to protest right-wing violence against immigrants, but the event is marred by

radical leftists thowing stones and eggs at President of Germany Richard von Weizsäcker and Chancellor of Germany Helmut Kohl.

- November 11 – The Church of England votes to allow women to become priests.
- November 13
  - The government of Peru announces it has arrested a small group of army officers who were plotting the assassination of President Alberto Fujimori.
  - A report by the World Meteorological Organization reports an unprecedented level of ozone depletion in both the Arctic and Antarctic.
  - Boxer Riddick Bowe defeats Evander Holyfield to become undisputed heavyweight champion.
- November 15 – The Lithuanian parliamentary election sees the Communists of the Democratic Labour Party of Lithuania, led by Algirdas Brazauskas, return to power.
- November 18 – Russian President Boris Yeltsin releases the flight data recorder (FDR) and cockpit voice recorder (CVR) of KAL 007, shot down by the Soviets in 1983.
- November 20 – In England, a fire breaks out in Windsor Castle, causing over £50 million worth of damage.
- November 24
  - In the People's Republic of China, a China Southern Airlines domestic flight crashes, killing all 141 people on board.
  - Elizabeth II describes this year as an *annus horribilis* (horrible year), due to various scandals damaging the image of the Royal Family, as well as the Windsor Castle fire.
  - The first commercial worldwide release in the videogame industry, nicknamed "Sonic 2sday", celebrates the release of the sequel to Sonic the Hedgehog, with an international release day event for the now best selling Sega Genesis game, Sonic the Hedgehog 2.
- November 25
  - *Disney's Aladdin* is released in theaters everywhere.
  - The Czechoslovakia Federal Assembly votes to split the country into the Czech Republic and Slovakia, starting on January 1, 1993.

- In a national referendum related to abortion, voters in Ireland reject the proposed Twelfth Amendment of the Constitution Bill, 1992 (Ireland) but approve the Thirteenth Amendment of the Constitution of Ireland and the Fourteenth Amendment of the Constitution of Ireland.
- November 27 – The government of Venezuela announces that it has put down a coup attempt by a group of army officers who bombed the presidential palace.
- November 30
  - The trial of 14 South Vietnamese accused of murdering 24 North Vietnamese begins in Hong Kong (ends November 29, 1994).
  - Secretary-General of the United Nations Boutros Boutros-Ghali encourages the United Nations Security Council to pass United Nations Security Council Resolution 794, authorizing military intervention in the Somali Civil War to allow emergency food supplies to reach the people of Somalia. The Council passes the resolution on December 3, and United States Marines begin arriving in Somalia on December 9.

December

- December 3
  - UN Security Council Resolution 794 is unanimously passed, approving a coalition of United Nations peacekeepers led by the United States to form UNITAF, tasked with ensuring humanitarian aid gets distributed and establishing peace in Somalia.
  - The Greek oil tanker *Aegean Sea*, carrying 80,000 tonnes of crude oil, runs aground in a storm while on approach to La Coruña, Spain, and spills much of its cargo.
  - The first SMS message is sent over the Vodafone GSM network in the United Kingdom.
- December 4 – U.S. military forces land in Somalia.
- December 6 – Extremist Hindu activists demolish Babri Masjid – a 16th-century mosque in Ayodhya, India, which had been used as a

temple since 1949, leading to widespread communal violence, including the Bombay Riots, in all killing over 1,500 people.

- December 7 – The United States wins the 1992 Davis Cup.
- December 8 – The last blast is fired at the Falun Mine in Falun, Sweden, after a millennium of continuous operation.
- December 9 – The Prince and Princess of Wales publicly announce their separation.
- December 12 – An earthquake hits Flores, Indonesia, leaving 2,500 dead.
- December 16 – The Czech National Council adopts the Constitution of the Czech Republic.
- December 18 – The South Korean presidential election is won by Kim Young-sam, the first non-military candidate elected since 1961.
- December 19 – State President of South Africa F. W. de Klerk dismisses or suspends 23 military officers, including 6 generals, on suspicion of unauthorized activities designed to disrupt negotiations with the African National Congress.
- December 20 – The Folies Bergère music hall in Paris, France, closes.
- December 21
  - A Dutch DC-10, flight Martinair MP 495, crashes at Faro Airport, killing 56 people.
  - President of Serbia Slobodan Milošević defeats Milan Panić in the Serbian presidential election.
- December 22 – The Archives of Terror are discovered by Dr. Martín Almada, detailing the fates of thousands of Latin Americans who had been secretly kidnapped, tortured, and killed by the security services of Argentina, Bolivia, Brazil, Chile, Paraguay, and Uruguay. This is known as Operation Condor.
- December 24
  - President-elect Bill Clinton names the final members of his cabinet.
  - President George H. W. Bush pardons 6 national security officials implicated in the Iran–Contra affair, including Caspar Weinberger.

- December 27 – A U.S. F-16 Fighting Falcon shoots down an Iraqi MiG-25 Foxbat that violated the Iraqi no-fly zones.
- December 29 – Brazil's president Fernando Collor de Mello is found guilty on charges that he stole more than $32 million from the government, preventing him from holding any elected office for 8 years.
- December 31 – President Bush arrives in Somalia to spend New Year's Day with U.S. troops who are part of the Unified Task Force.

Date unknown

- First confirmed detection of extrasolar planets, with the discovery of several terrestrial-mass planets orbiting the pulsar PSR B1257+12, by Aleksander Wolszczan and Dale Frail.
- Deng Xiaoping accelerates market reforms to establish a socialist market economy in the People's Republic of China.
- Queensland introduces Freedom Of Information Laws.
- The Council for National Academic Awards, UK is wound up.
- The Hospital Chaplains' Fellowship joins with the National Association of Whole Time Hospital Chaplains to form the College of Health Care Chaplains in the UK.
- In terms of units sold, compact discs outsell audiocassettes for the first time in the United States.

Births

January

Maja Keuc

Jack Wilshere

Alden Richards

- January 1 – Jack Wilshere, English footballer

- January 2 – Alden Richards, Filipino actor, model, singer and television personality
- January 3 – Delphine Wespiser, French beauty pageant titleholder
- January 12 – Georgia May Jagger, English model
- January 14 – Nimue Smit, Dutch model
- January 15 – Valerie Abou Chacra, Lebanese actress, radio announcer, model and beauty pageant titleholder
- January 16
  - Diana Golbi, Israeli singer
  - Maja Keuc, Slovenian singer
- January 17 – Nate Hartley, American actor
- January 19
  - Logan Lerman, American actor
  - Mac Miller, American rapper
  - Shawn Johnson, American Olympic gymnast
- January 20 – Maria Harfanti, Indonesian social activist, pianist, and beauty pageant titleholder
- January 25 – Olivia Bonilla, American singer-songwriter and musician
- January 26 – Cassidy Lehrman, American actress
- January 27
  - Sam Barry, Irish tennis player
  - Connor Widdows, Canadian actor
- January 28
  - Hunter Renfroe, American baseball player
  - Simone Egeriis, Danish singer
- January 30
  - Tom Ince, English footballer
  - Matthew Werkmeister, Australian stage and television actor
- January 31
  - Christopher Nissen, Danish singer
  - Tyler Seguin, Canadian ice hockey player

February

Neymar

Avan Jogia

Taylor Lautner

Freddie Highmore

- February 1 – Kelli Goss, American actress
- February 5
  - Neymar, Brazilian footballer
  - Kejsi Tola, Albanian singer
- February 7 – Maimi Yajima, Japanese singer
- February 8 – Karle Warren, American actress
- February 9
  - Valentina Barron, Australian actress
  - Ana Yorkira Binet, Dominican volleyball player
  - Darya Melnikova, Russian actress
  - Avan Jogia, Canadian actor
- February 11 – Taylor Lautner, American actor
- February 14 – Freddie Highmore, English actor
- February 15 – Greer Grammer, American actress
- February 17 – Meaghan Martin, American actress
- February 18
  - Logan Miller, American actor and musician
  - Melinda Shankar, Canadian actress
- February 19 – Paulina Gaitán, Mexican actress
- February 20
  - Nastassja Burnett, Italian tennis player
  - Jarred Tinordi, American ice hockey player
- February 23 – Samara Weaving, Australian actress
- February 25
  - Max Aaron, American figure skater
  - Zahia Dehar, French lingerie designer

- February 26
    - Sean Abbott, Australian cricketer
    - Mikael Granlund, Finnish ice-hockey player
    - Ai Shinozaki, Japanese gravure idol and singer

March

Emily Osment

Kaya Scodelario

John Boyega

- March 2 – Charlie Coyle, American hockey player
- March 4
  - Jazmin Grace Grimaldi, daughter of Albert II, Prince of Monaco
  - Jared Sullinger, American basketball player
- March 6 – Momoko Tsugunaga, Japanese singer
- March 9 – María Eugenia Suárez, Argentine actress and model
- March 10 – Emily Osment, American actress and singer
- March 13
  - L, South Korean singer (Infinite), dancer and actor
  - George MacKay, English actor
  - Antoni Sarcevic, English footballer
  - Kaya Scodelario, English actress and model
- March 14 – Jasmine Murray, American singer
- March 15
  - Sosie Bacon, American actress
  - Mary Lou, American actress
- March 17
  - Eliza Bennett, British actress
  - John Boyega, British actor
- March 22 – Jessie Andrews, American pornographic actress
- March 23
  - Morgan Evans, Welsh rugby league player
  - Kyrie Irving, American-Australian basketball player
  - Vanessa Morgan, Canadian actress and singer
- March 26
  - Nina Agdal, Danish model
  - Haley Ramm, American actress
- March 28
  - Elena Bogdan, Romanian tennis player
  - Liam Hess, British actor
  - Sergi Gómez, Spanish footballer
- March 29 – Chris Massoglia, American actor
- March 30 – Enrique Gil, Filipino actor

April

Daisy Ridley

Amy Diamond

Doc Shaw

- April 4
  - Alexa Nikolas, American actress
  - Jacquelyn Jablonski, American model
  - Lucy May Barker, British stage and screen actress
  - Christina Metaxa, Cypriot singer-songwriter

- April 5 – Emmalyn Estrada, Canadian singer
- April 7 – Alexis Jordan, American singer and actress
- April 8 – Shelby Young, American actress
- April 10 – Daisy Ridley, English actress
- April 11 – Naya, Lebanese singer
- April 12
  - Giorgio Cantarini, Italian actor
  - Chad le Clos, South African swimmer
- April 13
  - Péter Bernek, Hungarian swimmer
  - Melodie Monrose, Martiniquais model
  - George North, Welsh rugby player
  - Paul Richardson, American football player
- April 14 – Oliver Bohm, Swedish ice hockey player
- April 15
  - Amy Diamond, Swedish pop singer
  - Richard Sandrak, Ukrainian bodybuilder
  - John Guidetti, Swedish footballer
- April 16 – Prince Sébastien of Luxembourg
- April 18 – Alexandra Adornetto, Australian novelist of *The Strangest Adventures* series
- April 21 – Gone Thursday, American singer and actor
- April 22
  - Robin van Helsum, Dutch fraudster
  - Joc Pederson, American baseball player
- April 23 – Syd tha Kyd, American singer, producer and DJ
- April 24 – Doc Shaw, American actor and rapper
- April 27
  - Keenan Allen, American football player
  - Allison Iraheta, American singer
  - James Duke Mason, American actor
- April 28 – Boxxy, American internet celebrity
- April 30
  - Kenny Agostino, American professional ice hockey player
  - Travis Scott, American recording artist, music producer and musician
  - Marc-André ter Stegen, German footballer

May

Grace Phipps

Olivia Culpo

Sam Smith

- May 1 – Lacey Banghard, English model
- May 4
  - Courtney Jines, American actress

- - Grace Phipps, American actress and singer
  - Ashley Rickards, American actress
- May 6
  - Baekhyun, South Korean singer (EXO)
  - Vanesa Gabriela Leiro, Argentine actress and singer
  - Jonas Valančiūnas, Lithuanian basketball player
- May 7 – Alexander Ludwig, Canadian actor
- May 8
  - Ana Mulvoy-Ten, British actress
  - Olivia Culpo, Miss Universe 2012 American beauty pageant titleholder
- May 10 – Charice Pempengco, Fili–ino singer
- May 11 – Christina McHale, American tennis player
- May 12 – Malcolm David Kelley, American actor
- May 14 – A.J. Saudin, Canadian film and television actor
- May 17 – Eric Jagielo, American baseball player
- May 18
  - Spencer Breslin, American actor
  - Brian Idowu, Russian athlete
  - Laurie Kingsbury, Canadian athlete
  - Kevin Mendy, French athlete
  - John Persson, Swedish athlete
  - Nina Petushkova, Russian figure skater
- May 19
  - Sam Smith, British soul singer
  - Eleanor Tomlinson, English actress
  - Heather Watson, British tennis player
  - Xiao Wen Ju, Chinese model
- May 20 – Enes Kanter, Turkish basketball player
- May 21
  - Hutch Dano, American actor
  - Olivia Olson, American actress and singer
- May 22 – Chinami Tokunaga, Japanese singer
- May 24 – Agustín Velotti, Argentine tennis player
- May 28 – Mira Gonzalez, American poet
- May 29 – Gregg Sulkin, British actor
-

- May 30
  - Harrison Barnes, American basketball player
  - Danielle Harold, English actress

June

Mario Götze

Daryl Sabara

Mohamed Salah

Oscar Taveras

Jennette McCurdy

- June 1 – Amanda Ware, Australian model
- June 3 – Mario Götze, German footballer
- June 4 – Dino Jelusić, Croatian singer
- June 6 – Hyuna, South Korean dance-pop idol, singer, dancer, rapper, designer, model.
- June 6 – Abbie Cobb, American Actress
- June 9 – Lucien Laviscount, British actor and recording artist
- June 10 – Kate Upton, American model and actress
- June 12
  - Allie DiMeco, American actress and instrumentalist
  - Philippe Coutinho, Brazilian footballer
- June 14 – Daryl Sabara, American actor
- June 15
  - Mohamed Salah, Egyptian footballer
  - Ben Smith, Naval Architect
- June 19 – Oscar Taveras, professional baseball player (d. 2014)

- June 20 – Sage the Gemini, American rapper
- June 21 – Carly Booth, Scottish golfer
- June 23
  - Kate Melton, American actress
  - Bridget Sloan, American artistic gymnast
- June 24
  - David Alaba, Austrian football player
  - Raven Goodwin, American actress
- June 25 – Jaden Schwartz, Canadian ice hockey player
- June 26
  - Melanie Amaro, American singer
  - Jennette McCurdy, American actress and singer
- June 29 – Adam G. Sevani, Armenian-American actor and dancer
- June 30 – Holliston Coleman, American actress

July

Selena Gomez

- July 3
  - Maasa Sudo, Japanese singer
  - Nathalia Ramos, Spanish actress and singer
- July 5 – Mirna Radulović, Serbian singer-songwriter (Moje 3)
- July 7
  - Toni Garrn, German model
  - Holly Hagan, English television personality
- July 8
  - Kelsey-Beth Crossley, English actress
  - Sky Ferreira, American singer, songwriter, model, and actress

- July 9 – Douglas Booth, English actor
- July 10
    - Kristin Allen, American acrobatic gymnast
    - Eva Lim, Dutch figure skater
- July 15 – Koharu Kusumi, Japanese singer
- July 20
    - Paige Hurd, American actress
    - Jordan Rodrigues, Australian actor
- July 21
    - Jessica Barden, English actress
    - Rachael Flatt, American figure skater
- July 22 – Selena Gomez, American actress and singer
- July 23
    - Danny Ings, English footballer
    - Diwakar Vaish,Indian roboticist, Inventor of the Mind Controlled Wheelchair
- July 28 – George Spencer-Churchill, Earl of Sunderland
- July 31
    - Kyle Larson, American racing driver

August

Demi Lovato

- August 1 – Austin Rivers, American basketball player
- August 2
    - Hallie Eisenberg, American actress
    - Charlie XCX, English singer

- August 3 – Karlie Kloss, American model
- August 4 – Tiffany Evans, American singer
- August 6 – Victor Silayan, Filipino actor and commercial model
- August 7 – Bobby Lynn Bryant, American boxer
- August 9 – Young Thug, American Rapper
- August 11 – Allisson Lozz, Mexican actress and singer
- August 12 – Cara Delevingne, British model and heiress
- August 16 – Diego Sebastian Schwartzman, Argentine tennis player
- August 18
  - Rebecca Brown, American actress and musician
  - Amy Willerton, British model. Miss Universe GB 2013
- August 20 – Demi Lovato, American singer and actress
- August 21
  - RJ Mitte, American actor
  - Bobi Mojsoski, Macedonian singer
  - Felipe Nasr, Brazilian race car driver
- August 25 – Miyabi Natsuyaki, Japanese singer
- August 26 – Hayley Hasselhoff, American actress
- August 27 – Kim Petras, German singer
- August 28 – Bismack Biyombo, Congolese basketball player
- August 31 – Holly Earl, English actress

September

Nick Jonas

Safura Alizadeh

- September 1 – Hyelim, Korean singer and rapper
- September 2
  - Konrad Abeltshauser, German professional ice hockey player
  - Michele Gumabao, Filipino volleyball player and television personality
- September 3 – August Alsina, American hip hop singer
- September 7 – Gizem Karaca, Turkish model
- September 9
  - Frencheska Farr, Filipina singer, model and dancer
  - Damian McGinty, Irish singer and actor
- September 11
  - Desireé Bassett, American guitarist and recording artist
  - Maria Gabriela de Faría, Venezuelan actress and singer
- September 12
  - Krishna Raj, Thrissur Kerala India
  - Connor Franta, American YouTuber and entrepreneur
- September 14 – Zico, South Korean rapper, songwriter, and producer
- September 15 – Camélia Jordana, French singer
- September 16
  - Nick Jonas, American singer-songwriter and actor
  - Jake Roche, British actor and singer (Rixton)
- September 18 – Amber Liu, American singer
- September 20 – Safura Alizadeh, Azerbaijani singer, actress and saxophonist

- September 21
  - Mariya Muzychuk, Ukrainian chess player
  - Chen, South Korean singer (EXO)
- September 22 – Philip Hindes, British cyclist
- September 24 – Jack Sock, American tennis player
- September 27 – Jake Burbage, American actor
- September 28
  - Skye McCole Bartusiak, American actress (d. 2014)
  - Keir Gilchrist, Canadian actor
  - Tyler Lockett, American football player
  - Koko Tsurumi, Japanese artistic gymnast
  - Mawra Hocane, Pakistani actress and model
- September 29 – Marina Antipova, Russian ice dancer
- September 30 – Ezra Miller, American actor

October

Josh Hutcherson

Bryce Harper

Stephan El Shaarawy

- October 1 – Drew Chadwick, American musician (Emblem 3)
- October 3 – Aina Hashimoto, Japanese singer, actress and voice actress
- October 4 – Shun Miyazato, Japanese actor and voice actor
- October 5
  - Eric Cabral, Canadian actor and voice actor
  - Hirotaka Chiba, Japanese actor and voice actor
  - Lais Ribeiro, Brazilian model
- October 6 – Rhyon Nicole Brown, American actress, singer, and dancer
- October 7 – Grace Bawden, Australian singer
- October 9 – Tyler James Williams, American actor
- October 10 – Gabrielle Aplin, English singer and songwriter
- October 12 – Josh Hutcherson, American actor
- October 13 – Aaron Dismuke, American voice actor
- October 14 – Savannah Outen, American singer
- October 15 – Vincent Martella, American actor and singer
- October 16 – Bryce Harper, American baseball player
- October 17 – Jacob Artist, American actor, singer and dancer
- October 19
  - Shihō, Japanese actress and model
  - Lil Durk, American rapper
- October 20 – Ksenia Semyonova, Russian Olympic gymnast
- October 22 – Sofia Vassilieva, American actress

- October 23 – Álvaro Morata, Spanish footballer
- October 24 – Thelma Fardin, Argentine actress
- October 25 – Kamie Crawford, American pageant titleholder
- October 27
  - Emily Hagins, American film director
  - Taiko Katono, Japanese actor and model
  - Stephan El Shaarawy, Italian footballer
  - Brandon Saad, American professional ice hockey player
- October 28
  - Lexi Ainsworth, American actress
  - Maria Borges, Angolan model
  - Jermaine Crawford, American actor
- October 29 – Jacqueline Jossa, English actress
- October 30 – Tequan Richmond, American actor, model, and rapper
- October 31 – Vanessa Marano, American actress

November

Wilfried Zaha

Nathan Kress

Miley Cyrus

- November 2 - Chelsea Davis, American gymnast
- November 5 – Odell Beckham Jr., American football player
- November 6 – Megan Meier, American suicide victim (d. 2006)
- November 7 – Christopher Tavarez, American actor, model and athlete
- November 10 – Wilfried Zaha, English footballer
- November 12 – Macey Cruthird, American actress
- November 15 - Minami Minegishi, Japanese singer and actress (AKB48 and no3b)
- November 18 – Nathan Kress, American actor
- November 21 – Conor Maynard, British singer
- November 23
  - Miley Cyrus, American actress and singer
  - Gabriel Landeskog, Swedish hockey player
  - EunB, South Korean singer (Ladies' Code) (d. 2014)
- November 25 – Ana Bogdan, Romanian tennis player
- November 27
  - Chanyeol, South Korean singer (EXO)
  - Tola Szlagowska, Polish singer
- November 28
  - Adam Hicks, American rapper, actor and dancer
  - Jake Miller, American rapper and songwriter
  - Mireia Lalaguna, Spanish actress, model, beauty queen and Miss World 2015
- November 30 – Dylan Smith, American actor

December

Bridgit Mendler

- December 1 – Caleb Shomo, American musician and record producer
- December 6 – TooSmooth, American singer, songwriter, musician, record producer, and entrepreneur
- December 8 – Katie Stevens, American singer
- December 12 – Chen Ruolin, Chinese diver
- December 14
    - Ryo Miyaichi, Japanese footballer
    - Tori Kelly, American singer and songwriter
- December 17 – Thomas Law, British actor
- December 18 – Bridgit Mendler, American actress, singer, musician and songwriter
- December 23 – Spencer Daniels, American film and television actor
- December 26 – Kätlin Aas, Estonian fashion model

Deaths

January

Judith Anderson

- January 1
  - Grace Hopper, American computer scientist (b. 1906)
  - George M. Ferris, American investment banker and philanthropist (b. 1893)
  - Edward Leslie Gray, politician and member of the Legislative Assembly of Alberta from Alberta, Canada (b. 1895)
  - Kenneth Emory, American anthropologist (b. 1897)
  - Josef R. Sheetz, American military commander during World War II (b. 1895)
  - Francis J. Field, philatelist and stamp dealer (b. 1895)
- January 2 – Virginia Field, British actress (b. 1917)
- January 3 – Judith Anderson, Australian actress (b. 1897)
- January 7 – Richard Hunt, American puppeteer (b. 1951)
- January 9
  - Bill Naughton, British playwright (b. 1910)
  - Hans Jenny (pedologist), soil scientist and expert on pedology (b. 1899)
- January 14 – Irakli Abashidze, Georgian poet, literary scholar and politician (b. 1909)
- January 17 – Frank Pullen, English business person and racehorse owner (b. 1915)

- January 18
    - Aleksandr Almetov, Soviet Olympic ice hockey player (b. 1940)
    - Theodore Leslie Futch, United States Army officer with the rank of Brigadier General (b. 1895)
- January 20 – Abdul Khalek Hassouna, Egyptian diplomat, 2nd Secretary-General of the Arab League (b. 1898)
- January 21 – Eddie Mabo, Australian Indigenous rights activist (b. 1936)
- January 22 – A. J. Antoon, American theater director (b. 1944)
- January 23
    - Freddie Bartholomew, British actor (b. 1924)
    - Ian Wolfe, American actor (b. 1896)
- January 26 – José Ferrer, Puerto Rican actor (b. 1912)
- January 27
    - Sally Hayfron, Wife of Robert Mugabe and first lady of Zimbabwe (b. 1933)
    - Gwen Ffrangcon-Davies, British actress and centenarian (b. 1891)
- January 29 – Willie Dixon, American composer and musician (b. 1915)
- January 31 – Mel Hein, American football player (New York Giants) and member of the Pro Football Hall of Fame (b.1909)

February

Ray Danton

Jânio Quadros

- February 2 – Bert Parks, American game show host (b. 1914)
- February 3 – Junior Cook, American musician (b. 1934)
- February 4 – Lisa Fonssagrives, Swedish model (b. 1911)
- February 8 – Stanley Armour Dunham, Grandfather of US President Barack Obama (b. 1918)
- February 10 – Alex Haley, American author (b. 1921)
- February 11 – Ray Danton, American actor (b. 1931)
- February 12 – Bep van Klaveren, Dutch boxer (b. 1907)
- February 13 – Dorothy Tree, American actress (b. 1906)
- February 15 – William Schuman, American composer (b. 1910)
- February 16
  - Jules Gros, Breton linguist specializing in popular language (b. 1890)
  - Angela Carter, English novelist and journalist (b. 1940)
  - Jânio Quadros, 22nd President of Brazil (b. 1917)
  - Abbas al-Musawi, Lebanese Shia cleric and Secretary General of Hezbollah (b. 1952).
- February 20
  - Dick York, American actor (b. 1928)
  - Roberto D'Aubuisson, Salvadorean Army officer and right-wing political leader (b. 1944)
  - A. J. Casson, member of the Canadian group of artists known as the Group of Seven (b. 1898)
  - Eugene R. Black, Sr., American banker, former president of the World Bank (b. 1898)

- February 23 – Markos Vafiadis, Greek Communist leader (b. 1906)
- February 26 – Ettie Mae Greene, American supercentenarian (b. 1877)
- February 29 – Buddy O'Grady, American basketball player and coach (b. 1920)

March

Menachem Begin

John Ireland

- March 2 – Sandy Dennis, American actress (b. 1937)
- March 3 – Robert Beatty, Canadian actor (b. 1909)
- March 4
  - Néstor Almendros, Spanish cinematographer (b. 1930)
  - Art Babbitt, American animator (b. 1907)
- March 5 – Pare Lorentz, American filmmaker (b. 1905)
- March 9 – Menachem Begin, 6th Prime Minister of Israel, recipient of the Nobel Peace Prize (b. 1913)
- March 11
  - László Benedek, Hungarian film director (b. 1905)
  - Richard Brooks, American film director (b. 1912)
  - Liu Geping, Chinese politician (b. 1904)

- March 13 – Joseph Anderson, secretary to the First Presidency of The Church of Jesus Christ of Latter-day Saints (b. 1889)
- March 14 – Jean Poiret, French actor, screenwriter, director (b. 1926)
- March 16 – Yves Rocard, French nuclear physicist (b. 1903)
- March 17 – Jack Arnold, American TV and film director (b. 1912)
- March 18 – Antonio Molina, Spanish singer (b. 1928)
- March 19 – Cesare Danova, American actor (b. 1926)
- March 20 – Georges Delerue, French composer (b. 1925)
- March 21
  - John Ireland, American actor (b. 1914)
  - Natalie Sleeth, American composer (b. 1930)
- March 23 – Friedrich Hayek, Austrian economist, Nobel Prize laureate (b. 1899)
- March 25 – Nancy Walker, American actress (b. 1922)
- March 26 – Barbara Frum, Canadian journalist (b. 1937)
- March 28 – Nikolaos Platon, Greek archaeologist (b. 1909)
- March 29 – Paul Henreid, Austrian-born actor (b. 1908)
- March 30 – Manolis Andronikos, Greek archaeologist (b. 1919)

April

Isaac Asimov

Benny Hill

Satyajit Ray

Francis Bacon

- April 2
  - Juan Gómez González, *Juanito*, Spanish footballer (b. 1954)
  - Jan van Aartsen, Dutch politician (b. 1909)
- April 4
  - Samuel Reshevsky, seven-time U.S. Chess Champion (b. 1911)
  - Vintilă Horia, Romanian writer (b. 1915)
- April 5
  - Nawab Zulfikar Ali Khan, Indian Royal- Titular Nawab of Rampur; Indian politician and army major (b. 1933)
  - Suada Dilberović, Bosnian medical student. First casualty of the Siege of Sarajevo (b. 1968)
  - Molly Picon, American actress (b. 1898)
  - Sam Walton, American businessman, founder of Wal-Mart (b. 1918)
- April 6 – Isaac Asimov, Russian-born author (b. 1920)

- April 7 – Ace Bailey, Canadian hockey player (b. 1903)
- April 8 – Daniel Bovet, Swiss-born pharmacologist, recipient of the Nobel Prize in Physiology or Medicine (b. 1907)
- April 10
  - Peter D. Mitchell, British biochemist, recipient of the Nobel Prize in Chemistry (b. 1920)
  - Sam Kinison, American comedian (b. 1953)
- April 11 – Alejandro Obregón, Colombian painter (b. 1920)
- April 13 – Feza Gürsey, Turkish mathematician and physicist (b. 1921
- April 14
  - David Miller, American film director (b. 1909)
  - Sammy Price, American pianist and bandleader (b. 1908)
- April 16 – Neville Brand, American actor (b. 1920)
- April 19
  - Frankie Howerd, British comedian and actor (b. 1917)
  - Kristen French, Canadian murder victim (b. 1976)
- April 20 – Benny Hill, British comedian and actor (b. 1924)
- April 23
  - Czesław Zbierański, Polish engineer, pioneer of Polish aviation, major of Polish Army (b. 1885)
  - Satyajit Ray, Indian filmmaker (b. 1921)
  - Elmer Allison, American socialist political activist and newspaper editor (b. 1883)
  - Tanka Prasad Acharya Nepalese politician, former Prime Minister (b.1912)
- April 25 – Yutaka Ozaki, Japanese songwriter (b. 1965)
- April 27
  - Olivier Messiaen, French composer (b. 1908)
  - Louise de Kiriline Lawrence, naturalist, author and nurse (b. 1894)
- April 28 – Francis Bacon, Irish-born painter (b. 1909)
- April 29 – Mae Clarke, American actress (b. 1910)

May

Marlene Dietrich

Karl Carstens

- May 3 – George Murphy, American actor and politician (b. 1902)
- May 4 – Gregor Mackenzie, British Labour Party politician (b. 1927)
- May 5 – Adriana Admiraal-Meijerink, Dutch olympic fencer (b. 1893)
- May 6 – Marlene Dietrich, German actress (b. 1901)
- May 8 – Otto Šimánek, Czech actor (b. 1925)
- May 10 – John Lund, American actor (b. 1911)
- May 12 – Robert Reed, American actor (b. 1932)
- May 13
  - Gisela Elsner, German writer (b. 1937)
  - F. E. McWilliam, Northern Irish sculptor (b. 1909)
- May 14
  - Lyle Alzado, American football player (b. 1949)
  - Nie Rongzhen, Chinese Communist military leader (b. 1899)
- May 17 – Lawrence Welk, American musician (b. 1903)
- May 18
  - Janusz Kruk, Polish musician (b. 1946)
  - Jake Leicht, American athlete (b. 1919)
  - Skip Stephenson, American actor and comedian (b. 1940)

- o Marshall Thompson, American actor (b. 1925)
- May 21 – T. B. Ilangaratne, Sri Lankan author, dramatist, actor and politician (b. 1913)
- May 22
  - o Abraham Moles, French sociologist and psychologist (b. 1920)
  - o Tony Accardo, American gangster (b. 1906)
- May 23
  - o Atahualpa Yupanqui, Argentine singer, songwriter and guitarist (b. 1908)
  - o Giovanni Falcone, Italian judge (b. 1939)
  - o William Keene, American actor (b. 1915)
- May 25
  - o Philip Habib, Lebanese-American diplomat (b. 1920)
  - o Tulio Demicheli, Argentine film director (b. 1914)
- May 30 – Karl Carstens, former President of the Federal Republic of Germany (b. 1914)

June

Robert Morley

- June 2 – Philip Dunne, American screenwriter and director (b. 1908)
- June 3 – Robert Morley, English actor (b. 1908)
- June 4 – Carl Stotz, American founder of Little League Baseball (b. 1910)
- June 7 – Bill France, Sr., American founder of NASCAR (b. 1909)
- June 11 – Marjorie Newell Robb, Survivor of the sinking of RMS Titanic in 1912 (b. 1889)
- June 15 – Warren Prall Watters,ounding archbishop of the Free Church of Antioch (b. 1890)
-

- June 18
  - Carlos Humberto Perette, Argentinian politician, former Vice President (b. 1915)
  - Mordecai Ardon, Israeli painter (b. 1896)
  - Peter Allen, Australian singer, songwriter (b. 1944)
- June 19 – Kathleen McKane Godfree, British tennis player (b. 1896)
- June 21
  - Joan Fuster, Spanish writer (b. 1922)
  - Li Xiannian, former President of the People's Republic of China and one of the Eight Elders of the Communist Party of China (b. 1909)
- June 21 – Rudra Mohammad Shahidullah, Bangladeshi poet (b. 1956)
- June 22 – Chuck Mitchell, American actor (b. 1927)
- June 24 – Vera Griner, Russian rhythmitician (b. 1890)
- June 25
  - Jerome Brown, American football player (b. 1965)
  - James Stirling, British architect (b. 1926)
- June 26 – Buddy Rogers, American wrestler (b. 1921)
- June 27 – Allan Jones, American actor (b. 1907)
- June 28
  - Mikhail Tal, eighth World Chess Champion (b. 1936)
  - Guy Nève, racing driver (b. 1955)
- June 29
  - Mohamed Boudiaf, Algerian politician, president of the Republic (b. 1919)
  - Pierre Billotte, French Army officer and politician (b. 1906)

July

Brenda Marshall

Arletty

Leonard Cheshire

- July 2 – Camarón de la Isla, Spanish flamenco singer (b. 1950)
-

- July 4
  - Ástor Piazzolla, Argentine tango composer (b. 1921)
  - Francis Perrin, French nuclear physicist (b. 1901)
- July 5 – Paul Hackman, Canadian musician (b. 1953)
- July 9 – Eric Sevareid, American journalist (b. 1912)
- July 10
  - Albert Pierrepoint, British executioner (b. 1905)
  - Doris Tate, American campaigner for the rights of crime victims (b. 1924)
- July 11 – Deng Yingchao, Chinese Communist politician, widow of Zhou Enlai (b. 1904)
- July 12 – Florence McClung, American painter, printmaker, and art teacher (b. 1894)
- July 13
  - Alex Wojciechowicz, American football player (Detroit Lions) and member of the Pro Football Hall of Fame (b. 1915)
  - Cicely Williams, Jamaican physician (b. 1893)
- July 14 – Giuseppe Prezzolini, Italian literary critic, journalist, editor and writer (b. 1882)
- July 15 – Hammer DeRoburt, first President of Nauru (b. 1922)
- July 16 – Buck Buchanan, American football player (Kansas City Chiefs) and member of the Pro Football Hall of Fame (b. 1940)
- July 18
  - Rudolph Ising, cartoon animator (b. 1903)
  - Mordecai Ardon, Israeli painter. (b. 1896)
- July 19
  - Allen Newell, computer scientist (b. 1927)
  - Paolo Borsellino, Italian judge (b. 1940)
- July 22 – John Meyendorff, Russian-born Orthodox scholar (b. 1926)
- July 23
  - Rosemary Sutcliff, British author (b. 1920)
  - Suleiman Frangieh, Lebanese statesman, former President of the Republic (b. 1910)
- July 24 – Arletty, French singer and actress (b. 1898)
- July 25 – Alfred Drake, American actor (b. 1914)

- July 26 – Mary Wells, American singer (b. 1943)
- July 27 – Anthony Salerno, American mobster (b.1911)
- July 30
  - Brenda Marshall, American actress (b. 1915)
  - Joe Shuster, Canadian-American comic book artist (b. 1914)
- July 31 – Leonard Cheshire, English war hero and philanthropist (b. 1917)

August

Rob Muldoon

- August 3
  - Wang Hongwen, Chinese Communist politician (b. 1935)
  - Bertil Ohlin, Swedish economist and politician (b. 1899)
- August 4
  - František Tomášek, Czech Catholic cardinal (b. 1899)
  - Seichō Matsumoto, Japanese writer and journalist (b. 1909)
- August 5
  - Rob Muldoon, former Prime Minister of New Zealand (b. 1921)
  - Jeff Porcaro, American musician (b. 1954)
- August 6 – Simcha Bunim Alter, the fifth Rebbe of the Hasidic dynasty of Ger (b. 1898)
- August 7
  - Francisco Fernández Ordóñez, Spanish politician, former Foreign minister (b. 1930)
  - Lilo Milchsack, German promoter of Anglo-German relations (b. 1905)

- August 8
  - Abu al-Qasim al-Khoei, Iranian-Iraqi Shia ayatollah and scholar (b. 1899)
  - Alison Gertz, American AIDS activist (b. 1966)
- August 9 – Fereydoun Farrokhzad, Iranian entertainer (b. 1936)
- August 10 – Annisteen Allen, American blues singer (b. 1920)
- August 12 – John Cage, American composer (b. 1912)
- August 16 – Mark Heard, American singer (b. 1951)
- August 18
  - John Sturges, American film director (b. 1911)
  - Keith Henderson, Scottish painter (b. 1911)
  - Christopher McCandless, American itinerant and hiker, Starvation (b. 1968)
- August 19 – Curtis M. Scott, American role-playing game designer (birth unknown, age 32)
- August 22 – Hallowell Davis, American physiologist, otolaryngologist and researcher (b. 1896)
- August 28 – Tan Qixiang, Chinese historian (b. 1911)
- August 29 – Teddy Turner, English actor (b. 1917)

September

Barbara McClintock

- September 1
  - Morris Carnovsky, American actor (b. 1897)
  - Piotr Jaroszewicz, Polish politician, former Prime Minister (b. 1909)
- September 2 – Barbara McClintock, American geneticist, recipient of the Nobel Prize in Physiology or Medicine (b. 1902)
- September 4 – John van Dreelen, Dutch actor (b. 1922)
-

- September 5
  - Billy Herman, American baseball player (Chicago Cubs) and member of the MLB Hall of Fame) (b. 1909)
  - Fritz Leiber, American author (b. 1910)
- September 6 – Mervyn Johns, distinctive Welsh film and television character actor (b. 1899)
- September 12
  - Anthony Perkins, American actor (b. 1932)
  - Ruth Nelson, American actress (b. 1905)
  - Hans F. Koenekamp, American special effects artist and cinematographer (b. 1891)
- September 18 – Princess Margaret of Denmark (b. 1895)
- September 21 – Bill Williams, American actor
- September 25 – César Manrique, Spanish artist (b. 1919)
- September 29 – Paul Jabara, American actor, singer, and songwriter (b. 1948)

October

Willy Brandt

- October 4 – Denny Hulme, New Zealand race car driver (b. 1936)
- October 5 – Eddie Kendricks, American singer (b. 1939)
- October 6 – Denholm Elliott, English actor (b. 1922)
- October 7 – Tevfik Esenç, last known speaker of Ubykh (b. 1904)
- October 8 – Willy Brandt, Chancellor of Germany, recipient of the Nobel Peace Prize (b. 1913)
- October 11 – Choi Sae-hwang, South Korean lawyer and Vice-Minister of Defense (b. 1919)

- October 12
  - John Hancock, American actor (b. 1941)
  - Ulysses Guimarães, Brazilian politician (b. 1916)
- October 16 – Shirley Booth, American actress best known for playing the title character in the television series *Hazel* (b. 1898)
- October 17
  - Yoshihiro Hattori, Japanese exchange student (b. 1975)
  - Herman Johannes, Indonesian professor, scientist and politician (b. 1912)
- October 19
  - Arthur Wint, Jamaican Olympic runner (b. 1920)
  - Gert Bastian, German politician (b. 1913)
  - Petra Kelly, German politician (b. 1947)
- October 21 – Jim Garrison, American attorney (b. 1921)
- October 22
  - Red Barber, American sportscaster (b. 1908)
  - Cleavon Little, American actor (b. 1939)
- October 24 – Laurie Colwin, American author (b. 1944)
- October 25
  - Roger Miller, American singer (b. 1936)
  - Adelino da Palma Carlos, Portuguese politician, former Prime Minister (b. 1905)
- October 27 – David Bohm, American-born physicist, philosopher, and neuropsychologist (b. 1917)
- October 31 – Gary Rippingale, English ice hockey player (b. 1974)

November

Alexander Dubček

- November 2 – Hal Roach, American director and producer (b. 1892)
- November 4
  - George Klein, Canadian inventor (b. 1904)
  - José Luis Sáenz de Heredia, Spanish film director (b. 1911)
- November 5 – Jan Oort, Dutch astronomer (b. 1900)
- November 7
  - Alexander Dubček, Slovakian politician, former First Secretary of the Communist Party of Czechoslovakia (b. 1921)
  - Jack Kelly, American actor (b. 1927)
  - Richard Yates, American writer (b. 1926)
- November 10 – Chuck Connors, American actor (b. 1921)
- November 11 – Earle Meadows, American Olympic athlete (b. 1913)
- November 19 – Diane Varsi, American actress (b. 1938)
- November 21 – Kaysone Phomvihane, Laotian statesman and Communist Party leader, president of the Republic (b. 1920)
- November 22 – Sterling Holloway, American actor (b. 1905)
- November 23
  - Roy Acuff, American singer (b. 1903)
  - Mohamed Benhima, former Prime Minister of Morocco (b. 1924)
- November 25 – Joseph Arthur Ankrah, Ghanaian military office, former head of the State (b. 1903)
- November 26 – John Sharp, English actor (b. 1920)
- November 27 – George M. Ferris, American investment banker and philanthropist (b. 1893)
- November 29
  - Emilio Pucci, Italian fashion designer (b. 1914)
  - Jean Dieudonné, French mathematician (b. 1906)
- November 30 – Peter Blume, American painter and sculptor (b. 1906)

December

Dana Andrews

Peyo

- December 1 – Esau Khamati Oriedo, Kenyan of African ancestry; an anti-colonialism activist and crusader (b. 1888)
- December 2 – Michael Gothard, British actor (b. 1939)
- December 3
  - Luis Alcoriza, Mexican film director (b. 1918)
  - Nureddin al-Atassi, Syrian Baathist, former President of the Republic (b. 1929)
- December 6
  - Mimi Smith, maternal aunt and guardian of John Lennon (b. 1906)
  - Percy Herbert, English actor (b. 1920)
- December 7
  - Jean Bell Thomas, American festival promoter (b. 1881)
  - Richard J. Hughes, American politician, 45th Governor of New Jersey, and Chief Justice of the New Jersey Supreme Court (b. 1909)

- December 9 – Vincent Gardenia, Italian-American actor (b. 1920)
- December 10 – Celia Gámez, Argentinian actress (b. 1908)
- December 12
  - Ali Amini, Iranian politician, former Prime Minister of Iran (b. 1905)
  - Suzanne Lilar, Belgian essayist, novelist and playwright (b. 1901)
- December 17 – Dana Andrews, American actor (b. 1909)
- December 18 – Mark Goodson, American game show producer (b. 1915)
- December 21
  - Stella Adler, American acting teacher (b. 1901)
  - Nathan Milstein, Ukrainian-born violinist (b. 1903)
  - Albert King, American musician (b. 1923)
- December 22
  - Frederick William Franz, a member of the Governing Body of Jehovah's Witnesses and 4th President of Watch Tower Bible and Tract Society (b. 1893)
  - Ted Willis, British television dramatist and author (b. 1914)
- December 23 – Eddie Hazel, American guitarist (b. 1950)
- December 24 – Pierre Culliford, *Peyo*, Belgian comics artist, creator of *The Smurfs* (b. 1928)
- December 25
  - Ted Croker, English former football official (b. 1924)
  - Monica Dickens, English author (b. 1915)
  - Jules Gros, Breton linguist specializing in popular language (b. 1890)
- December 26 – Nikita Magaloff, Georgian-Russian pianist (b. 1912)
- December 29 – Vivienne Segal, American actress (b. 1897)

Date unknown

- Luigi Stipa, Italian aeronautical, hydraulic, and civil engineer and aircraft designer (b. 1900)

Nobel Prizes

Nobel medal

- Physics – Georges Charpak
- Chemistry – Rudolph A. Marcus
- Medicine – Edmond H. Fischer, Edwin G. Krebs
- Literature – Derek Walcott
- Peace – Rigoberta Menchú
- Economics – Gary Becker

In the News

The first Nicotine patch is introduced to help stop smoking.

Turkey, an earthquake registering 6.8 on the Richter scale kills over 500.

Mafia boss John Gotti is sentenced to life in prison.

McDonalds opens first McDonalds in Beijing China.

Euro Disney opens in France.

Bill Clinton becomes U.S. president.

IRAQ Continues to hamper the efforts of UN Weapons Inspectors.

Fire damages a major part of Windsor Castle.

The Summer Olympics are held in Barcelona, Spain.

Mike Tyson Convicted of the Rape Miss Black Rhode Island, Desiree Washington.

Following the public outcry over royal spending the Queen of England will now pay income tax.

Rioting breaks out in Los Angeles following the acquittal of four white police officers accused of beating black motorist Rodney King.

Windows 3.1 released by Microsoft.

Space Shuttle Endeavour makes successful maiden voyage.

Popular Films - Aladdin, Home Alone 2: Lost in New York, Batman Returns, Lethal Weapon 3, A Few Good Men, Sister Act, The Bodyguard, Wayne's World, Basic Instinct, Unforgiven, Honey, I Blew Up The Kid, Reservoir Dogs.

www.ingramcontent.com/pod-product-compliance
Lightning Source LLC
Chambersburg PA
CBHW060644290526
45793CB00001B/386